WILD WILD WORLD

COCKROACHES

by Liza Jacobs

BLACKBIRCH®
PRESS

San Diego • Detroit • New York • San Francisco • Cleveland • New Haven, Conn. • Waterville, Maine • London • Munich

Photographs © 1998 by Li wen-kuei

Cover photograph © Corel

© 1998 by Chin-Chin Publications Ltd.

No. 274-1, Sec.1 Ho-Ping E. Rd., Taipei, Taiwan, R.O.C.
Tel: 886-2-2363-3486 Fax: 886-2-2363-6081

LIBRARY OF CONGRESS CATALOGING-IN-PUBLICATION DATA

Jacobs, Liza.
    Cockroaches / by Liza Jacobs.
        v. cm. -- (Wild wild world)
    Includes bibliographical references.
    Contents: Cockroaches -- Food -- Enemies -- Kinds.
    ISBN 1-4103-0047-1 (hardback : alk. paper)
    1. Cockroaches--Juvenile literature. [1. Cockroaches.] I. Title. II.
Series.

    QL505.5.J23 2003
    595.7'28--dc21
                                                        2003001464

Printed in Taiwan
10 9 8 7 6 5 4 3 2 1

Table of Contents

About Cockroaches 4

Night Creatures 6

Food 8

Mating 10

Eggs 12

Babies 14

Growing and Molting 16

Escaping Enemies 18

Survival Experts .20

Changing and Growing 22

For More Information 24

Glossary 24

About Cockroaches

Cockroaches lived on this planet long before dinosaurs roamed the earth! A cockroach is an insect. There are thousands of different kinds of cockroaches. They live all over the world.

Like all insects, the body of a cockroach has three main parts. It has a head, a thorax (midsection), and an abdomen (rear section).

Cockroaches have large compound eyes. Compound eyes are made up of hundreds of tiny eyes.

Cockroaches have four feelers next to their mouth. They also have two long antennae on their heads. Most cockroaches have two pairs of wings, but they do not fly very often.

Like all insects, cockroaches have three pairs of legs. Stiff hairs poke out from their legs and help them sense movement.

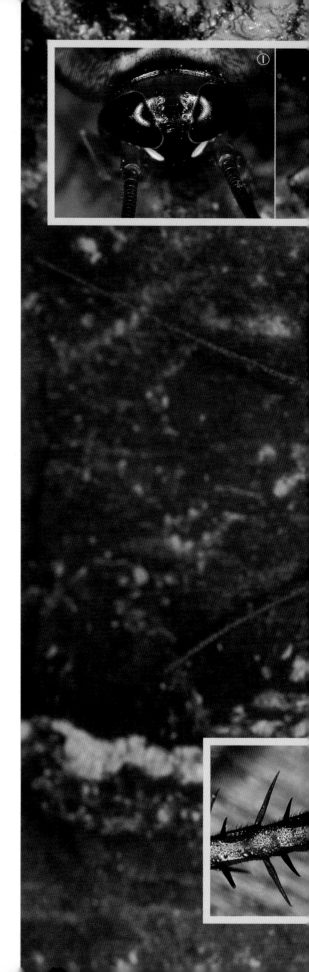

Night Creatures

Cockroaches spend most of the day sleeping and staying out of sight. Some keep to themselves, while others gather in groups. The flat shape of a cockroach's body helps it slip through cracks and hide in small places.

At night, cockroaches come out to search for food. They use their sensitive antennae to help them smell and touch. Their mouth feelers are used for tasting food before eating. This way, a cockroach can tell what is safe to eat. A cockroach has sharp jaws filled with teeth for crunching and chewing up food.

Food

What do cockroaches eat? Almost anything! They eat plants, wood, insects, animal droppings, and dead animals. They even eat other cockroaches! These bugs will also eat any pet food or human food they can find: soap, paper, clothing, glue—the list goes on! Cockroaches also need to drink a lot of water.

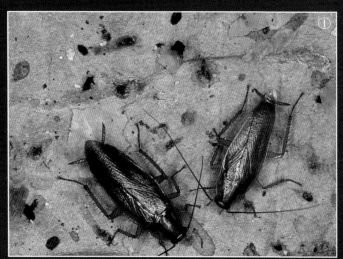

Mating

Some types of cockroaches only mate once or twice during their life. Other kinds mate many times. When a female cockroach is ready to mate, her body gives off a smell that attracts male cockroaches. Once she has chosen a partner, the two cockroaches mate by connecting their back ends.

Eggs

Most cockroaches deposit eggs in an
egg case. (One type of cockroach gives
birth to live young.) Some carry the egg
case under their abdomen for a while.
Others drop the case right away.

A female usually finds a safe place to leave her egg
case, such as the underside of a leaf, in a pile of
wood, or in a dark corner. Most females do not stay to
raise their young. The babies grow inside the egg case
until it is time for them to hatch.

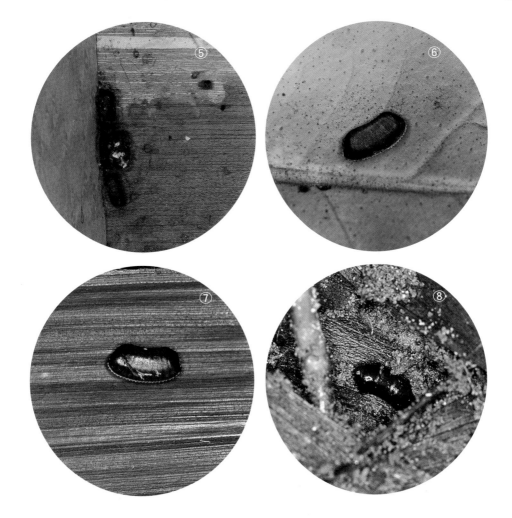

Babies

Baby cockroaches are called nymphs. When the nymphs are ready to hatch, they swallow air to puff up their bodies. This helps the egg case split open. One by one, the babies wriggle out. Their bodies look a lot like adult cockroaches. But unlike adults, the nymphs do not have wings.

Insects have a hard covering over their bodies called an exoskeleton. When a nymph first hatches, its exoskeleton is clear. It darkens during the next few days.

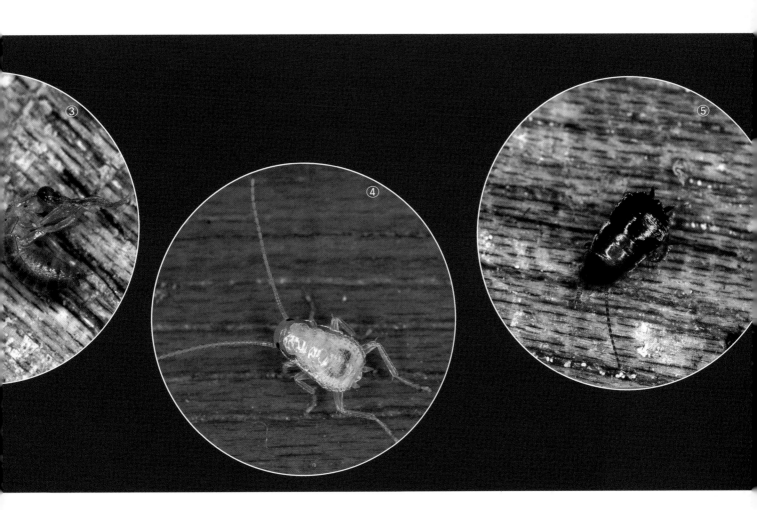

Growing and Molting

Like other insects, a cockroach's exoskeleton does not get bigger as the insect grows. In order to grow to its adult size, a cockroach has to shed its exoskeleton. This is called molting.

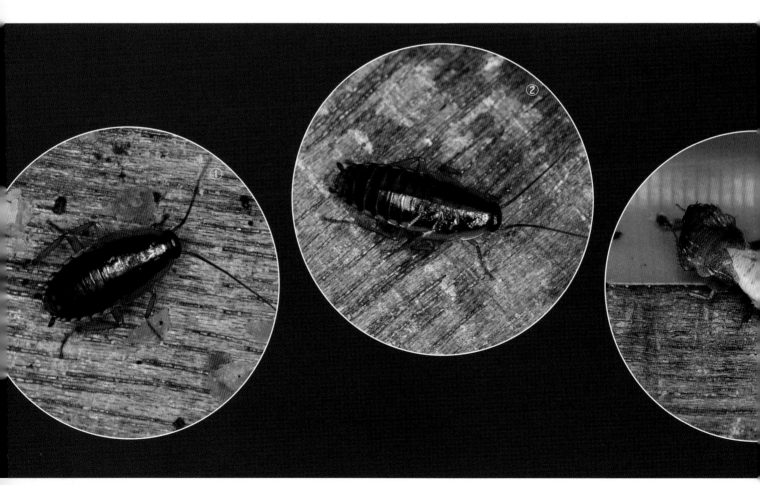

Underneath the old covering, is a new one! It is soft at first, but quickly hardens. Cockroaches molt between 6 and 12 times. By the time a cockroach has completed its last molt it is fully grown and has developed wings.

Escaping Enemies

There are many kinds of animals that eat
cockroaches. Frogs, toads, lizards, mice,
birds, and snakes all eat cockroaches.
Spiders, scorpions, centipedes, and other
kinds of insects eat them, too.

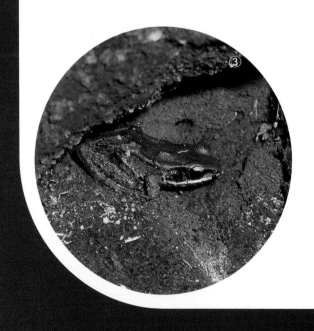

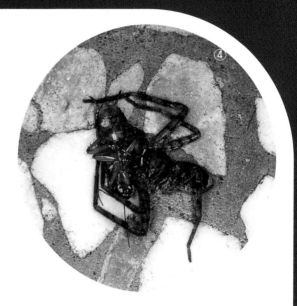

A cockroach, however, has many ways of escaping attack. Its sensitive feelers tell it when danger is nearby. Cockroaches are extremely fast runners. And they have a bad smell that makes some enemies run the other way!

Survival Experts

Cockroaches are found in a wide range of sizes and colors. Some have interesting spots, stripes, or other patterns on their bodies.

Cockroaches are known to crawl inside homes, restaurants, and other buildings where people live. In these places, they are thought of as pests. But most cockroaches live outside. They live in forests, deserts, mountains, and grasslands. They can survive almost anywhere.

Changing and Growing

Many insects go through major changes as they grow into their adult forms. These changes are called metamorphosis. Some types of insects, such as caterpillars, go through complete metamorphosis. These insects look nothing like their adult form at the beginning of their lives. They go through four stages—egg, larva, pupa, and adult.

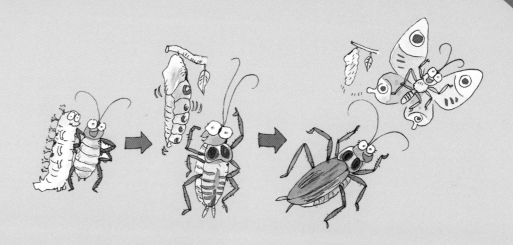

Other insects, such as grasshoppers and cockroaches, go through incomplete metamorphosis. These are insects that look like small adults when they hatch from their eggs. To change into their adult form and develop wings, these insects molt several times.

For More Information

Brimner, Larry Dane. *Cockroaches.*
Danbury, CT: Childrens Press, 1999.

Merrick, Patrick. *Cockroaches.* Mankato,
MN: Child's World, 2003.

Rustad, Martha. *Cockroaches.* Mankato, MN:
Pebble Books, 2003.

Glossary

compound eye an eye that has many lenses

exoskeleton the hard covering on the outside of an insect's body

metamorphosis changes an insect's body goes through as it
grows from birth to its adult form

molt to shed the outer skin or covering

nymph a baby cockroach